# Between Heaven and Earth

By Kelly Chripczuk

Kelly Chripczuk
321 West 1st St.
Boiling Springs, PA 17007
www.thiscontemplativelife.org

Book Layout © 2017 BookDesignTemplates.com

Between Heaven and Earth  -- 1st ed.
ISBN 978-1-9795567-8-1

*For the beauty of the earth,*
*For the glory of the skies,*
*For the love which from our birth,*
*Over and around us lies,*
*Lord of all, to thee we raise,*
*This our hymn of grateful praise.*

—HYMN BY F. S. PIERPOINT

# Contents

## Earth

# *Introduction*

*"The material world is wedded to the immaterial . . . the gift of language allows us to span the gap between the two."*
- in *Chicken Scratch: Stories of Love, Risk, & Poultry*

"Between Heaven and Earth" is a collection of poems written between 2012 and 2017. The poems are roughly divided into three sections. The first section, Heaven, contains poems based on biblical passages. Many were written as part of my sermon preparation process.

The last section, Earth, contains poems that grew out of concrete experiences of daily life. These poems are loosely arranged around the season in which they were written.

The middle section, Between, contains poems that explore the more ambiguous intersections of heaven and earth. In this space of convergence, often filled with darkness and mystery, true identity is both held and formed.

*Heaven*

# Coaxing the Fire

*[God] breathed into his nostrils the breath of life;*
*and the man became a living being. Gen.2:7*

The wood is slow
to burn this morning,
reluctant and stubborn.
Leaning into the stove's
metal mouth, I draw
deep breaths and
exhale with force,
keeping a steady rhythm.

This must be
how God hovered
over the still body
formed from the earth,
the slow, stubborn
dust pressed together.

God leaning,
breathing,
and the human
bursting into life,
like a flame;
God coaxing
the fire
of humanity.

# I Was Afraid

*I was afraid . . . and I hid . . . Genesis 3; Matt. 25*

The old habit dies hard,
the fear that drives one
like a hare, hunted, pursued
by God-only-knows what terror,
darkened shadow, lurking nightmare.

I was afraid, Adam said, because I was naked.
Vulnerable, exposed, like the soft clay he once was
before God's great hand scooped mud from mud,
molding in intricate detail the figure of humanity.
Oh Adam, God sighed.  God's hands hung low and lifeless,
weary, at the great heaving sides, heart-broken,
heavy.  Adam's flesh tingled at the sight of those hands,
at the thought of their touch, but he mistook his longing
for fear and later, his descendants would do the same
when God came, clothed in flesh and mud and walked among
them, God's great hands hidden in human form.

I was afraid, the servant said, his one talent held in an
outstretched, shaking hand.  I knew you were a harsh man . . .
so I hid.  Memory played the scene as he spoke, the anxious
weight of the coin in his hand, the feeling that it watched - the
Master watched - through the coin's cold, unblinking eye.  The
waiting and absence, the dread, too much to bear.  He fled in
the night, carrying the coin into darkness where, still, the moon
caught and glimmered on gold.  Half-crazed, he dug,
with bare hands, a hole.  It was not the coin he wanted to hide,
but himself.  Clay and dirt clung to his hands, lodged under
his fingernails, the damp earth claiming him as its own.

After, he fled the spot.  Still, the coin's light shone
in his mind's eye, pressing after him in the dark.

We are a people forever misinterpreting the light, the presence.
The habits of fear and hiding, buried deep in our DNA.  Still, God
pursues.  The words, Where are you? echo, as God, the great,
love-sick lover, with hands gentle as they are wide, seeks a
people made of earth and clay.

# A Word May Come

*Isaiah 30:21*

When you lie wide awake
in your bed, unable to sleep,
you might remember
a line you used to know
by heart.

Whether it rises or descends,
I cannot say, only this: you will
know its arrival by the quiet hum
of recognition that strikes
like heat lightening,
quiet and bright.

Then, you must go
to sleep.  In the morning,
the word will still be there
running straight through
the heart of you,
like the needle
of a compass.

You will know, again,
the way.  All that remains
is to walk in it.

## Some Mornings

*O, that you would tear open the heavens and come down . . .*
*– Isaiah 64:1*

Some mornings, the mountains
disappear completely, blanketed
by a wall of white that divides the distance
between presence and sight.

Maybe this is what Isaiah saw,
this barrier, this great divide.
Then he, a lover maddened by desire,
cried out without thinking,
"Tear open the heavens
and come down!"

Isaiah burned with longing,
his coal-singed lips tingled,
and God, whose passion simmers
long and slow, was aroused
by the pining of his people.

Then, God came forth
as a tiny seed, conceived
by earth's desire, born
in the rending wide
of heaven's door.

## The Hardest part

*I slept but my heart was awake.  Listen!  My beloved is knocking.*
*- Song of Solomon 5:2*

*. . . you know what time it is, how it is now the moment for you*
*to wake from sleep.  - Romans 13:11*

They come to our room in the night,
nose dripping blood or underwear damp.
"Can you help me with this?" they ask,
and we are stirred from the heavy
darkness of slumber.

I never want to wake in the night,
never want to throw back the warm covers,
to search for glasses blindly.
I dread the wet sheets
and sitting in the cold dark of the bathroom
pinching his nose until the red river stops.

But when he shivers, stripping the wet
in exchange for dry, or when he waits
oddly stoic for the clotting to begin,
I feel compassion rise.

By the time I tuck them
back in, I can say I love you and
mean it as I rub their short-cropped hair.

The hardest part is waking.

# The Visitation

*Luke 1:39-56*

A small seed of fear planted itself
in the base of her throat
the moment the angel arrived.
Longing and love allowed the words, "Let it be,"
to squeeze past the lump.  Then, "the thing
with feathers/ that perches in the soul"
alighted in her breast and there the two
– fear and hope – dwelled together.

Who can say which aided her more
as her feet hurried along the path
to Elizabeth's house – fear that pressed
her from behind, or hope that drew
her like a flame?

It was the sight of Elizabeth,
that wizened woman rising
with effort to her feet, her great,
round belly swaying its eager path
toward Mary, that broke the tie.

Mary laughed at the sight - a short, sharp
bark bursting past fear,
dislodging it forever,
like a watermelon seed
spit on a summer afternoon.

Mary laughed, like Sarah had.
The sound grew, and her lips spread wide,
revealing white teeth and red tongue
and Elizabeth, catching the glimmer
in Mary's eye, began to sing and sway
in a strange dance, made absurd
by her swollen belly and ripening old age.
Mary giggled, like the young girl she was,
like someone who had nothing left to lose
and everything to gain.

Elizabeth's own face expanded
in joy and wonder as she grasped Mary's
hands and looked into her eyes.
This is when, the story goes, young
John leaped his famous leap, but it's also
the moment in which the thing with feathers
sprouted wings and sprung from Mary's soul —
hope flew up her throat, past her parted lips,
bursting into song.

Mary's words winged their way over and between
the two women as they swayed and spun together,
two bodies met in expectancy.

# John the Baptist

*Luke 1:41, Mark 1:4-8, 6:14-29*

He didn't see it, but felt it
through the darkness
of his mother's womb.
The flame that baptized
drew close enough
to singe his foot,
causing him to leap.

That wild fire caught
and grew, ruining him
for a life of conformity.
He moved to the wilderness,
somewhere near the river's edge.
Others were drawn
to his smoldering flame
and he doused them each with water,
warning them of the fire to come.

Later, when he leapt
from this world to the next,
(leaving his head behind),
he was greeted by the fellowship
of the flame – Isaiah
with his charred black lips,
Miriam who danced
like a flickering wick,
and others, too many to name.

Together, they glowed like
so many embers, a growing flame,
lighting the long, dark night.

# The Animals on Christmas Eve

*. . . she laid him in a manger . . . Luke 2:7*

Legend claims,
at midnight
Christmas Eve,
animals received
the gift of speech.

But, I imagine
it was the other way around
that first starlight night.

Animals didn't gain,
but humans lost,
for once,
their words.

Speechless,
they welcomed
the Word in silence,
led by the animals
in a chorus of mute wonder.

# Midnight Benediction

*Behold, I am bringing you good news of great joy. Luke 2:8-14*

Half-awake,
deep under layers of blankets,
I hear him cry out
in his cold, dark room
at the end of the hall.

"Ya-yuh?  Ya-yuh!" he calls,
pausing to wait for his brother's reply.
Answering silence is followed by thump, patter,
then the squeak of his door.
Half-way down the hall,
the word, "Mommy" slips from his lips.

"What?" I call, still snuggled, waiting to hear
what will be required of me.
A drink of water?
A blanket straightened and tucked?
A song or a hand held in the dark?

"I love you," he calls, then turns,
hurrying back to his warm bed.

Now I am awake and thinking
of his voice splitting the night
like an angel choir, the words,
"I love you" falling like snow
across an otherwise silent night.

# After

*Matt. 2:1-12*

After you find the One for whom you wait,
after you are overwhelmed with joy,
and kneel to kiss holy ground,
you might also find yourself
returning home by another road.

The ways you once walked may no longer
appeal.  Though the way now is dark
and takes you further 'round,
you will know at once it is your road,
the path for which you were made.

# Healing at the Pool of Bethesda

*John 5:1-9*

How long must you wait
by the water's edge
for the angel to dip
her fickle toe and
stir the surface
of the world?

And what if,
even after
days, months
of waiting,
watching,
you sense
the air's movement,
see the water shimmer
with circle after concentric
circle and yet,
are unable
to enter in?

To be near
the miracle is not
enough.  Second
place will earn you
no reward.

What then?

Nothing, then, can move
you, save for the one
question most difficult,
"What do you want?"

The answer
to that question
turns you away
from waiting,
away from the still,
smooth, surface
of the water.

The answer
to that question
bids you, "Pick up
your mat and walk."

# God Sleeps

*Mark 4:35-41*

God sleeps, yes,
but not like we do.

God sleeps
like a mountain:
tall, majestic,
home to streams
that run, rushing
down his face,
home to deer
that wander,
home to the hiker who stops
on the trail midway
between valley and peak.

God sleeps, yes,
but not like we do.

God tosses and turns
like an old man dreaming,
a tangled mass
of what was,
what is,
what will be.

God sleeps and is silent,
while the storm rises
and with it panic.

God sleeps like ocean
depths unruffled by wind.

'Wake up!' we cry, 'Wake up!'

The earth shudders,
the mountain quakes,
the old man sighs and turns in his sleep,
the ocean calms around us.

# Filled With Compassion

*While he was still far off, his father saw him and was filled with
compassion . . - Luke 15:20*

First comes divestment,
the division of all you have,
blessed, broken, and given,
like bread.

Then the wait begins,
the long, empty hours and days
wherein you wander the vacant
halls of your life, emptied
of all that owned you.

Your life is a bowl now,
open, hollowed out,
exposing a breadth
and depth of love,
a willing humility.

Then, and only then,
will you be filled
with compassion,
filled with that which reaches out
beyond the borders of you,
beyond emptiness,
to embrace
one come home.

## To the Older Brother

*Now his elder son was in the field . . . Luke 15:25*

"You are not a slave."
That is what I wanted
to say to you when I saw
you standing in the field.
And I ran out
to you
also.

# To Experience Resurrection

*John 20:1-9*

You have to return to the tomb
to experience resurrection.
Return to the place where once
you knew without doubt
all hope was gone, the last
dying gasp of breath expelled.
Return to silence and
the great tearing open
of sky and earth.

The first sign of spring
is the revelation of winter's
destruction.  Snow's clean
slate hides decay.  But,
when the sun's warmth rises,
it discloses a depth
of loss – the grass,
brown and trampled, barren
broken limbs scattered, earth
exposed and the empty stretch
of field filled with brown stalks
of decomposition.

This is the time of waiting,
the time in which we grow
weary and lose heart.

You have to watch sleeping

soil, pull back brown leaves,
lean close scanning hidden
places.  You have to stand beside
the stone, Martha would tell us,
your trembling hand pressed against
its cold, hard surface.  You have to enter
the dark cave, Peter whispers, not knowing
what you'll find.

You have to sit through the long,
dark night to see the first light of morning,
to feel the sharp intake of breath
as the sky's closed eye, cold and gray
cracks open slowly, then with growing
determination.  This is what you must do
to experience resurrection.

# Between

# You

You are not the ocean -
not the wind that moves across,
not the crashing waves,
nor the glassy ease as evening falls.

You are not the clear blue,
the emerald green, the angry waves,
gray and white.  You are not the silver
school of fins spinning
in synchronized motion, nor
the great beasts that lurk and glide.

You are something smaller –
the silent oyster resting on the deepest floor.

But, again, you are not the oyster,
nor its opening or closing,
but something smaller yet.
You are the pearl, opalescent,
that dwells within, smooth and still.

You are the pearl.

Because of this,
you are all of these things and more –
the ocean, the wind, the waves,
the creatures great and small,
the oyster, and the pearl.

# The Woods

Within you dwells a wood.
In it, are trails – some old and overgrown,
others fresh-cut and, between them, wide
spaces tangled with untamed growth.

In those woods you are every age
you have ever been, every age you will be.
Those woods walk up the mountain and down
the other side; those woods go on forever.

In those woods, ancient trees stand, sturdy,
scarred, and thick.  Those woods whisper
your name.  "Be who you are,"
they sigh, "that's all that was ever needed."

## The Center

You don't hold
the center,
it holds you.
Do you see
the difference?

It's not your job
to grasp and cling.
Yours is to rest,
aware.

Each sorrow,
each joy, is a
passing breeze
swaying the
hammock
that holds you.

## I Am

I am both:
the sunflower
and the seed.

Both: turning
toward the light
and digging
down, deep
into darkness.

There is not
one without
the other.

# Half Moon Heart

My heart is
a half moon peaking
out of a mid-day sky.

There is more, always more,
hidden; more than I can
know or see.

Lord, teach me to tend,
carefully, the shadow
places where deep
roots dwell.

Teach me to love,
tenderly, the cool
darkness, to prize it
along with the light.

## This Thread, These Crumbs

I want to explain
how it feels:
it seems my life
is held together
by an unseen thread,
a shimmering strand
of gossamer, perhaps.

As I pass through each
moment in time and space,
I am forever looking for signs
of its presence.

Like Hansel and Gretel,
I walk hunched over,
peering through each day,
seeking, searching,
for the elusive crumbs
that lead through
these dark woods
toward home.

## Conversion

The way a snowflake melts
into a river – that's one
one way to explain it;

the way everything is changed,
yet, what was remains,
now part of something more.

# Echolocation

*ech-o-lo-ca-tion (noun): the location of objects by reflected sound, in particular that used by animals such as dolphins and bats.*

To be a person
of faith, is to consent
to life lived blind as a bat,
to be a people of light
walking in darkness.

Faith will teach you
what you need to know
about soaring at night,
listening for the echo
of your own prayers
reverberating back to you.

The way forward is revealed,
always, in relation to the
place where you are.

## Never Far

Sometimes, it seems
I've lost track of God;
like one might lose
a child in a crowd or
misplace the keys
to a car you drive
every day.

At this, God laughs.

God is not easily lost,
if ever.  God is never far.
God is as near, always;
like the misplaced glasses
perched on top of your head,
the car keys jangling in the pocket
of your favorite coat.

# Seeing In the Dark

*Isaiah 30:20*

I'm thinking of the wee,
tiny cubs, born
blind and helpless
in the dark
den of winter.
How is it that
they travel,
unseeing,
toward the
life-giving teat
in that small,
dark space?

What I mean,
is there must be
other ways of seeing,
of being led,
in darkness -
maybe scent or
some deeper intuition.

There must
be something
that tells
the lone cicada
to dig up,
not down,
something that

whispers to the child
in the womb
when the time
has come.

Maybe it's
the voice
that comes
from behind,
as the prophet says,
whispering
in one's ear,
"This is the way,
walk in it."

Whatever it is,
I'm looking
for that leading now.
Now that the lights
are out, I'm developing
every one of my senses.

## Night Will Hold You

When the grief you carry
wears your face into a thousand
lines, when sadness feels
like a knife splitting your body
in two, night will come, at last.

With the children tucked safe
in their beds, you will stand
in the doorway of your own
darkened room and night
will welcome you with its wide
and gentle embrace.

How can I explain that this
is what you need, what you
have waited for, this knowing
that the darkness is nothing
to fear?  You will lie down
on your bed, half curled
around the old, old wound,
with your face turned toward
the windows.  Weeping,
your eyes will search
outlines of trees, the few
bright stars captured in each
window's frame.

Now that you are no longer afraid,
the night will hold you with its velvet
love, the emptiness of the darkness

will sidle up against you as a well
of grief pours out.

"There's something comforting
about the darkness," you will tell
your husband when he finds you there.
Instinctively, like the night, he will curl
himself around you offering not words,
but himself to hold you, his own body
echoing the sweet, silent night
that draws you close.

# Earth

# Turn and Be Saved

Sometimes, all it takes
is the slight movement of your eye,
a tilt of your head, your heart, to admit
a new angle, to see a way out, a way through
that was always there, but just out of sight, like God is.

This can happen in the smallest pauses, like the rest
between inhale and exhale, or the moment just before
the words you might always regret make their way out
of your mouth.  This is the salvation we've been waiting for,
the one thing always given, if only we would turn and receive.

# When the Word is Hard

When the passage assigned
is hard and sharp,
solid, like stone,
I try to crack it with
my mind-vice.  Stuck,
I also apply the pressure
of commentaries - three -
each striking from different
angles.  When the passage
fails to yield (does it ever yield
under such force?) I turn it daily,
like a Rubik's cube.  I hunt, like the woman
who lost a coin, seeking a key to unlock
the good news.

(Too often, I am looking
for comfortable news, not good.)

When I wear myself out, when the words
wear me down, I decide at last to let it be.
I am the one who yields, who accepts: I
have been given these words, not others.
Then, the passage works on me, like water
on stone, until I am cracked open and somewhere
in the cool, dark, earthen heart of me the gospel
seed is planted and takes root.

# What Keeps Me

*. . . the doors of hell are locked on the inside. - C.S. Lewis*

What keeps me
from the joy and wonder
of this day, this moment,
is the dream, the longing,
to be in some other
place – a golden past,
a possible future, or
some alternate now.

I want so badly to escape
that I'm unwilling
to turn the key
of surrender,
to set myself free
by dropping into
what is, and so, I remain
locked apart, absent.

If, as Lewis said,
the doors of hell are locked
on the inside, maybe
life is one long
lesson in learning
to turn the key.

# The Longest Night

The journey down into
the well of grief is deep,
but there are gifts along
the way.

Bright and shining stones
line the path, guiding travelers
into the heart of things.
These appear, one-by-one
like stars across a darkening sky.

The journey is long, and the well
is deep, but these stones sustain.

## Morning Devotions

Kneeling on the cold stone
hearth each morning,
facing yesterday's ashes,
cold and gray as death,
ignites a necessary humility.
Today's fire must be made
from what lies at hand -

life and heat coaxed
from old newspaper,
kindling, and a match
arranged just so.  And
only one log waits in the
wood box, big enough
to snuff it all out.

You must face this possible
failure every day if you wish
to stave off the chill, to warm
the house before the children wake
in their innocence, unaware
of this wrestling with wood
and flame, unaware of
the effort it takes, the faith.

# Advent

The cat comes in
through the window after
his morning jaunt.  Fresh air
clings to his mane, and I
bury my face in the fluff
around his neck.

I believe this is also
how Christ comes
into our midst – soft
and sudden, squeezing
in among us, smelling
of earth and grass
and morning frost.

## Prayer, For Winter

Send us a Cardinal,
a bright visitor flitting
across the landscape of this
wide world that lies,
dimly lit and sleeping.

Send us a moment of beauty
to reawaken us, just one bright
messenger of Hope.

# There's Something to be Said

There's something to be said
for a shower that forces you
to kneel each morning,
like a flower bent
by heavy rain.
*   *

Alone, in a cold house
one evening on retreat,
I heated water for a bath.
I filled pots and a tea kettle
on the stove, and made trip
after trip up and down
two flights of stairs.
It took three rounds
just to get the tub lukewarm.

Watching myself,
I wondered whether
it was all a ruse, a
busy way of avoiding prayer,
but then again, maybe
the work - the commitment,
the longing for a good, long soak
- was itself a prayer.
*   *

Every morning now I genuflect,
knees on porcelain,
while warmth rains down on me.
There's something to be said for that.

# When the Wood is Wet

Shift each log.
Make room for air to move through.

Turn your head away and inhale, deep, through nostrils.
Then turn again toward the dark stove and exhale.
Aim low, for the coals, but not low enough to stir the ashes.
Blow out long and hard until all air is gone.

Repeat.  Again and again.  Listen for the roar,
watch for flames to leap.

Make each breath a prayer
for all the wet wood in your
weighted down life.  Breathe out
for you, your spouse, your children.
Beg the flames to rise
as you tend them.

Shifting each log,
making room for air to move through.

# Origami

I slide carefully crafted prayers
under heaven's door -
reasonable requests plainly scrawled
on flat, white sheets of paper.

These, God takes and turns,
fold by fold, into something new.

God sends my desires back to me
in the strangest guises - a flitting
bird, a bouncing frog - fullness of life
when I thought only to ask for provision.

## Holy Saturday's Work

(for that which is already, but not yet)

Go outside and kneel
beside still-sleeping beds.
Strip away all that's dead;
the leaves, brown and curled,
and the dry, empty stems
of last year's flowers.
Straighten, one-by-one,
the scallop-edged bricks
that have stood, leaning,
all year-long like forgotten
gravestones.  Roll the giant
flowerpot aside and wonder
at the sound of stone
scraping against stone.

## Spring Arrives

Dead mums staggered
in the flower bed outside
the kitchen window
and rattled their bones
at me all winter long.

Today, under a
warming sun,
I bent and broke
their brown branches
at the base where new
green leaves spoke
spring's surprise.

Then, I walked around
the house, surveying
winter's damages.
Like the disciples
returning to the tomb,
I found in death's bed
signs of life.

This never fails to
astonish me,
like Christ popping
through locked doors,
bright with light,
a daffodil.

## How It Has Always Been

*I am able to approach the Buddhas barefoot and undisturbed,*
*my feet in wet grass, wet sand. – Thomas Merton describing his*
*visit to the sleeping Budhas in the Asian Journal*

My son comes walking toward me, barefoot,
across the wet summer grass.
The morning light lays soft around him.
In that moment, I see how it is,
how every child is a contemplative,
exposed in every way to the Now.

"This is what you must become," Jesus whispers.
I see now how it has always been: God
and God's children, barefoot, the morning grass
cool and wet beneath their feet.

## Grandma's Chickadees

Grandma fed her chickadees
religiously, for years.  Filling
a rusted coffee can with sunflower
seeds, she loaded the feeder outside
her big picture window, daily.

Seated with binoculars and bird book in hand,
she watched the window like a big screen TV.
A .22 leaned casually against the window frame.
She slipped its nose out occasionally, firing a round
at marauding Blue Jays and other greedy types.

Her letters to me, in shaky script, described
birds she saw and bears; often
mother bears moving through the old
orchard on their way to the river
with cubs in tow.

She stopped shooting the rifle, she said,
after she accidentally shot a hole in the floor.
When a bold bear came and stood outside the window
making eye contact, she also stopped feeding the birds.

I wanted her to feed them anyway,
to stand her petite frame in the wide
window, binoculars in one hand and riffle
in the other, like a sharp shooter in the WWII
movies Grandpa and I watched in her
living room.  I wanted food for the birds,
which were food for her.  I wanted her to keep

feeding them.

Now I walk my own property
toting bags of oiled, black sunflower seeds.
One by one, I lower, fill, and rehang feeders.
I watch dumpy doves, dapper cardinals, bright yellow finches,
and the greedy squirrel who hangs upside-down by his toes.
I lift my children to face the window. "Look! See!" I say.

We're a long way from the mountains,
though I can see them in the distance.
I don't believe the bears will find me here,
but if they do, maybe I'll tell them
about my Grandmother – her binoculars and gun,
her happy, well-fed chickadees.

# Tell me Again

"Tell me again, Mommy, where does the shadows go?"

By morning's light, my love, as dawn creeps
over the mountain, I roll them up tight, every shape
that echoes an object.  I gather night's shadows,
soft like velvet, slipping smoothly through my hands,
and tuck them into the far corners of your closet
and behind the attic door.  All day long they wait,
deepening, seeping the smell of rich, dark
earth, of damp caves and mushroom spores.

When evening descends, and you're busy with dessert,
I roam the house, stretching shadows out again,
smoothing them flat across ceiling or floor,
these soft shapes of remembrance, the dark reminders
that what you cannot see does not cease to exist
when the lights go out.  Shadows lengthen, like faith,
as darkness descends.  Shadows remind us
to believe in things unseen.

# Bloodhound

Head-down, thick folds of skin slide forward to cover her eyes.
Long ears drag the ground and swing in time with every step,
as the scent of one just passed spirals up the length
of her nose.  Hard upon the trail of one she cannot see,
led by scent (also unseen), she bumps against old tree stumps
her hard head knocking with the force of her longing.

It's all forward rushing until the trail turns and pursuit shifts
to pause, discerning.  Then she's off again, certain in her
blindness.

It's neither day nor night, only Now
with the scent of God fresh all around.
She's the hound who hunts, everywhere
a fresh trail, every chase an arrival.

## Prayer, for Summer

God of the summer rain,
send us each a moment
of shaking laughter or tears
to crack open the dry, barren
land of our hopes deferred.

# My Grandmother's Lap

I sat on my grandmother's lap
in an old wooden pew.
The shiny pipe organ
breathed in and out and a man
in a long robe stood
at the front of the church.

Sometimes, children
were called to the front
and we sat on the floor,
gathered around the feet
of the man in the long robe.
We lined up like ducks, heads tipped
up, waiting for the hand that
scatters bread.

Back in the pew, in my Grandmother's lap,
summer's heat rose around me.  Light poured in
through stained glass windows
and my long brown hair clung to the back
of my neck.

My Grandmother's small hands, always
cool, lifted my hair, gently gathering it
up and to the side.  Then she blew her own
breath onto my exposed neck and air,
cool and fresh, like a mountain spring,
trickled across my skin.

*'Man cannot live on bread alone,'*

Jesus said and those hands, that breath,
were grace to my love-parched skin –
a simple act of comfort-given and received
while I sat in church, in a worn wooden pew,
balanced on the shore of my Grandmother's lap.

# I Hear a Voice

When fear creeps in, clinging,
I hear a voice say, "Open."

When I leave, by well-worn mental paths,
the time, the place, the space I'm in,
I hear a voice say, "Return."

When I watch the boys on bikes
chasing round and round the van
in the driveway, when I see my daughter
smile secretly at the dog in the yard,
I hear a voice say, "This is good."

When tears rise at the mere thought
of an act, when my heart somersaults
in my chest and the muscles of my legs
clench tight, I hear a voice say, "Pay attention."

This is the voice of knowing,
the voice that leans whispering
Truth.  "This is light.  This is darkness,"
the voice says, "It matters not where
you are, I am with you, always."

# About the Author

Kelly Chripczuk is a licensed pastor, spiritual director and writer who lives in Central PA with her husband and four children. Their 110 year old farm house is also home to an ever-changing menagerie of pets. She published her first book, *Chicken Scratch: Stories of Love, Risk, & Poultry* in 2016. When she isn't tending the woodstove, the yard, or the hens, Kelly writes regularly at www.thiscontemplativelife.org. She is also available for workshops and retreats.

Made in the USA
Las Vegas, NV
18 February 2022